the teacher's friend

"Note" book

**a complete record keeping system
for teachers to send notes
home to parents
with
50 two-part
carbonless forms
by
karen sevaly and harry truax**

**teacher's friend
publications**

Copyright © 1989

Teacher's Friend Publications, Inc.

All rights reserved.

Printed in the United States of America

Published by Teacher's Friend Publications, Inc.

3240 Trade Center Drive, Riverside, CA 92507

ISBN 0-943263-12-3

How to Use the Teacher's Friend "Note" book

Does this situation sound familiar? A student's behavior has driven you to your wit's end. You have called a joint conference with the student's parents and the principal. Just as the conference begins, the parent says, "I don't know why this problem has been allowed to develop this far. If only the teacher had told us, we could have taken action a long time ago." You gasp because you have sent home at least four notes over the past month.

Wouldn't it be great to reply, "But, you were notified. I've sent home four notes about this matter. Here are copies of the notes and your responses."

In the current atmosphere of teacher accountability and litigation, you need a copy of all correspondence. The **Teacher's Friend "Note"book** provides a complete record keeping system for all communications and is contained in one, easy-to-use, format.

The **Teacher's Friend "Note"book** contains fifty ready-to-use, carbonless forms. The white copy of each form is sent home to the parents. The yellow copy remains in the book as a handy reference guide and documentation. (Make sure that you fold the back cover under each set before writing to avoid damaging additional forms.)

You will notice that the yellow page has lines to help guide your handwriting. Always be careful to avoid spelling and grammatical errors. These errors are often used to discredit a teacher's competency. Examples of such errors often sidetrack the parent from the discipline issue and places the teacher on the defense.

Make your notes brief and to the point. Two lines appear at the bottom of the note. One is for your signature and the other can be used for the student's signature or the signature of an adult witness.

The bottom of the white page is for the parent's reply. When you receive the reply, simply staple it to your copy of the note sent home. The lower portion of the yellow page can be used to document additional actions taken by the teacher.

Sample notes and suggestions are included on the following pages.

The Discipline Note

When writing a Discipline Note, follow these rules:

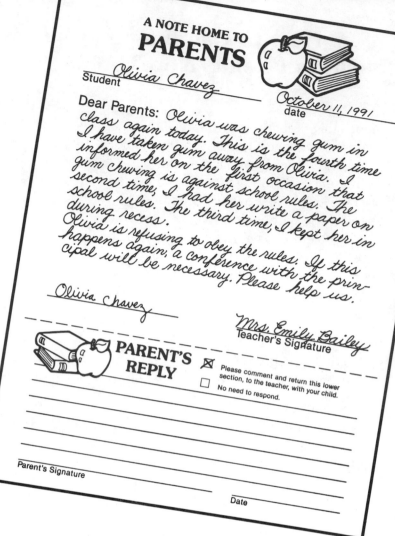

A NOTE HOME TO
PARENTS

Student _Olivia Chavez_

Dear Parents: *Olivia was chewing gum in class again today. This is the fourth time I have taken gum away from Olivia. I informed her on the first occasion that gum chewing is against school rules. The second time, I had her write a paper on school rules. The third time, I kept her in during recess. Olivia is refusing to obey the rules. If this happens again, a conference with the principal will be necessary. Please help us.*

date *October 14, 1991*

Olivia Chavez

Mrs. Emily Bailey
Teacher's Signature

PARENT'S REPLY

☒ Please comment and return this lower section, to the teacher, with your child.

☐ No need to respond.

Parent's Signature

Date

- Cool down! Never send a note home in anger. If you write one, keep it overnight and reread it before sending it home with the student.

- Avoid appearing to be personally offended toward the student or the situation. Never use the phrases, "I don't like...," or "I'm angry because..."

- Assume a professional viewpoint in your writing. Emphasize your concern that the child develop good values and citizenship. The infringement of classroom rules is important but not as significant as the child's development.

- Make sure that you list the disciplinary steps you have taken.

- Enlist the parent's help. This is a good time to ask for their cooperation and assistance.

- Be clear and concise about the actual problem. In the example, the problem is not really gum chewing, which would be a minor infraction. The real problem is the defiance of authority.

It is important to have the student sign the note as part of the disciplinary procedure. It also verifies that the note was given to the student to take home. This is actually more efficient than mailing the note home, as some students have been known to watch the mailbox. Often times, letters from school mysteriously disappear in the mail. If you do not receive a reply back from the parent in a day or two, make a phone call.

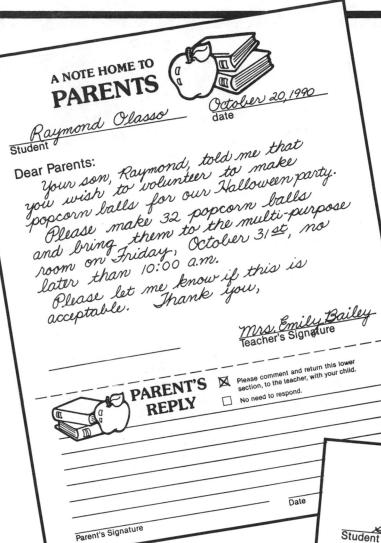

A NOTE HOME TO PARENTS

Student: *Raymond Olasso*

date: *October 20, 1990*

Dear Parents:

Your son, Raymond, told me that you wish to volunteer to make popcorn balls for our Halloween party. Please make 32 popcorn balls and bring them to the multi-purpose room on Friday, October 31st, no later than 10:00 a.m.

Please let me know if this is acceptable. Thank you,

Mrs. Emily Bailey
Teacher's Signature

PARENT'S REPLY

☒ Please comment and return this lower section, to the teacher, with your child.

☐ No need to respond.

Date _____

Parent's Signature

The Information Note

The Information Note must answer the important questions, who, what, where and when. If Mrs. Olasso, in the example, shows up with only fifteen popcorn balls at noon, your note will show that you did give the correct information. A request for a reply will verify that Mrs. Olasso understands the instructions and explains that she was volunteered by her son, Raymond.

The Health Report Note

The parent often sees the Health Note as an accusation of child negligence. Always use tact and be nonjudgmental The best approach is to be "matter of fact," and emphasize that the problem is a common one.

Of course, if genuine child abuse is suspected, don't send a note, notify the proper authorities.

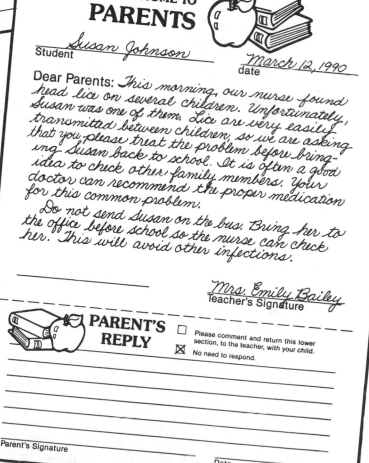

A NOTE HOME TO PARENTS

Student: *Susan Johnson*

date: *March 12, 1990*

Dear Parents: *This morning, our nurse found head lice on several children. Unfortunately, Susan was one of them. Lice are very easily transmitted between children, so we are asking that you please treat the problem before bringing Susan back to school. It is often a good idea to check other family members. Your doctor can recommend the proper medication for this common problem.*

Do not send Susan on the bus. Bring her to the office before school so the nurse can check her. This will avoid other infections.

Mrs. Emily Bailey
Teacher's Signature

PARENT'S REPLY

☐ Please comment and return this lower section, to the teacher, with your child.

☒ No need to respond.

Parent's Signature

Date _____

The Accident Note

The Accident Note has two purposes. One purpose is to notify the parent of a situation. The secondary purpose is to protect yourself from claim of negligence. The example note clearly shows that the student broke school rules when she was injured. It also points out that proper first aid was given. Include a second signature, that of an adult witness, in case the note is not delivered. Always request a parental reply to make sure that the parents know about the accident and for confirmation about the parents' follow through. It is also a good idea to follow up with a evening phone call. (Make a note, on the yellow copy, of the telephone conversation or your attempt to make the call.)

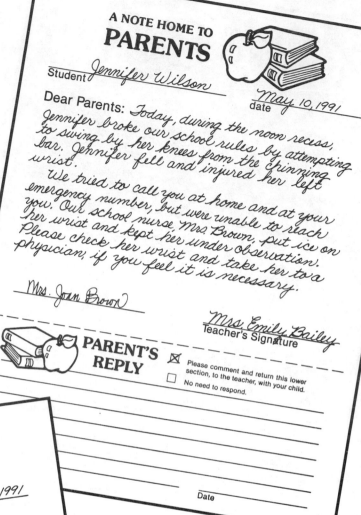

A NOTE HOME TO **PARENTS**

Student _Jennifer Wilson_

May 10, 1991
date

Dear Parents: Today, during the noon recess, Jennifer broke our school rules by attempting to swing by her knees from the chinning bar. Jennifer fell and injured her left wrist.

We tried to call you at home and at your emergency number, but were unable to reach you. Our school nurse, Mrs. Brown, put ice on her wrist and kept her under observation. Please check her wrist and take her to a physician, if you feel it is necessary.

Mrs. Joan Brown

Mrs. Emily Bailey
Teacher's Signature

PARENT'S REPLY

☒ Please comment and return this lower section, to the teacher, with your child.
☐ No need to respond.

Date

A NOTE HOME TO **PARENTS**

February 24, 1991
date

Billy Jenkins
Student

Dear Parents:
Billy hasn't turned in any math homework this week. He now has four "zeros" in the gradebook. Billy also scored a failing grade on the last math test.

Billy needs your help at home. Please contact me for a conference so we can both help Billy before he fails math this grading period.

I am available after school on Mondays or Wednesdays between 3:00 and 4:00 p.m.

Mrs. Emily Bailey
Teacher's Signature

Billy Jenkins

PARENT'S REPLY

☒ Please comment and return this lower section, to the teacher, with your child.
☐ No need to respond.

Date

Parent's Signature

The Academic Note

The purpose of the Academic Note is to avoid a very common complaint by parents, "Why didn't anyone tell me Billy was having a problem?" Make sure that you have the student sign the note as proof that it was given to him to take home.

At parent conference time, your copy of the note sent home will verify that you carried out your responsibility.

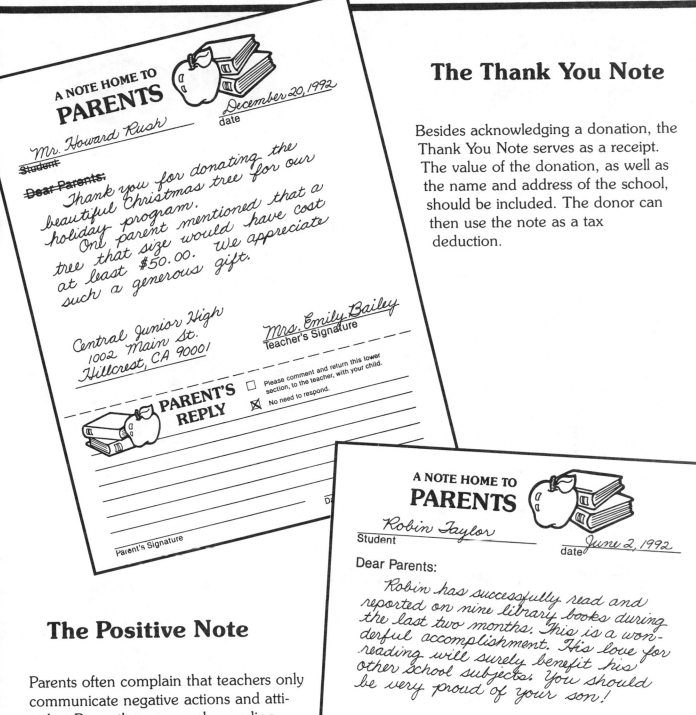

A NOTE HOME TO PARENTS

Mr. Howard Rush
~~Student~~

date December 20, 1992

~~Dear Parents:~~

Thank you for donating the beautiful Christmas tree for our holiday program.

One parent mentioned that a tree that size would have cost at least $50.00. We appreciate such a generous gift.

Central Junior High
1002 Main St.
Hillcrest, CA 90001

Mrs. Emily Bailey
Teacher's Signature

PARENT'S REPLY
☐ Please comment and return this lower section, to the teacher, with your child.
☒ No need to respond.

Parent's Signature

The Thank You Note

Besides acknowledging a donation, the Thank You Note serves as a receipt. The value of the donation, as well as the name and address of the school, should be included. The donor can then use the note as a tax deduction.

A NOTE HOME TO PARENTS

Robin Taylor
Student

date June 2, 1992

Dear Parents:

Robin has successfully read and reported on nine library books during the last two months. This is a wonderful accomplishment. His love for reading will surely benefit his other school subjects. You should be very proud of your son!

Mrs. Emily Bailey
Teacher's Signature

PARENT'S REPLY
☐ Please comment and return this lower section, to the teacher, with your child.
☒ No need to respond.

Parent's Signature   Date

The Positive Note

Parents often complain that teachers only communicate negative actions and attitudes. Prove them wrong by sending a complimentary note home when a student has reached a major goal or accomplishment. In the example, Robin's parents will see that you do acknowledge the good points in their child. This is especially important if Robin has received discipline notes in the past.

The Interdepartment Note

The Interdepartment Note is helpful when you want a copy of a note to verify that you notified the right person about a problem. In the example, the note confirms that informing the custodian of the situation was not effective. Your note to Mr. Jones, the principal, should receive prompt attention. If action is still not taken, you are protected if a child is injured.

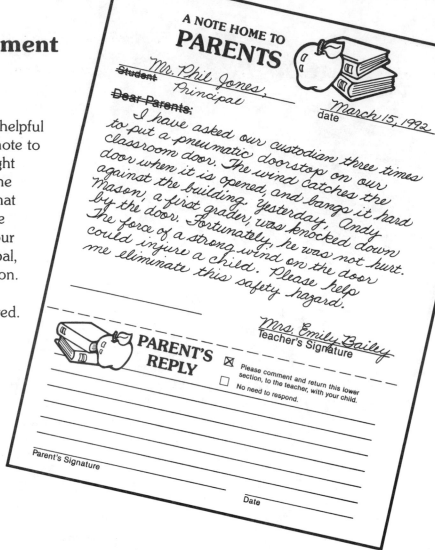

A NOTE HOME TO
PARENTS

~~Student~~ Mr. Phil Jones,
Principal

~~Dear Parents:~~   March 15, 1992
                                                          date

I have asked our custodian three times to put a pneumatic doorstop on our classroom door. The wind catches the door when it is opened, and bangs it hard against the building. Yesterday, Andy Mason, a first grader, was knocked down by the door. Fortunately, he was not hurt. The force of a strong wind on the door could injure a child. Please help me eliminate this safety hazard.

Mrs. Emily Bailey
Teacher's Signature

PARENT'S REPLY

☒ Please comment and return this lower section, to the teacher, with your child.
☐ No need to respond.

Parent's Signature

Date

Use your **Teacher's Friend "Notes"** whenever you foresee a need for a copy. The need for filing the notes, which wastes valuable time, is eliminated. In addition, the copies are available chronologically in the book for quick reference. When all of the forms have been used, simply file the book away and purchase a new one.

Many school principals wisely require a copy of all notes to parents be filed in the school office. With **The Teacher's Friend "Note"book** your copy will be available to you and your principal. When you need to verify your actions, your **"Note"book** will truly be a precious friend as well as an effective, time-saving tool.

Last of all, save your copies of **Teacher's Friend "Notes."** They will be an invaluable source when you write your autobiography!

DESCRIPTIVE WORDS TO USE IN WRITING NOTES HOME TO PARENTS

Discipline Words

accountable	imprudent
adversary	inappropriate
agitate	incident
antagonistic	incite
attitude	incivility
argumentative	incompatible
authority	inconsiderate
behavior	incorrigible
belligerent	indignant
challenge	ineffective
condescend	ineligible
confiscation	inflexible
contemptuous	inharmonious
contrary	immature
defensive	insensitive
defiant	insubordinate
deliberate	insulting
destructive	intentional
deterrent	intimidating
disagreeable	intolerant
discord	irresponsible
discourtesy	malice
disobedient	malicious
disorderly	misbehave
dispute	offensive
disrespectful	obstinate
disruptive	privilege
dissident	profane
frequent	prohibitive
frustrating	provoked
hostile	quarrel
ill-mannered	refusal
ill-tempered	remark
impatient	resistant
impolite	rude
impressionable	selfishness
improper	unacceptable

Positive Words

achievement	high standards
accomplishment	honorable
accurate	humble
adaptable	impressive
admired	improvement
advantage	independent
agreeable	influence
character	informative
complete	ingenious
competent	initiate
complementary	insight
confident	inspire
congenial	integrity
conscientious	intelligent
considerate	mastered
consistent	meticulous
content	mature
cooperative	optimistic
credible	obedient
courteous	proficient
decisive	profound
dependable	polite
effective	receptive
efficient	respective
effort	responsible
enjoyable	self-control
excellence	self-esteem
exemplary	sincere
expedient	substantial
expertise	successful
flexible	superb
grateful	talented
guidance	thorough
harmonious	trustworthy
helpful	

Academic Words	Health Words	Accident Words
accountable	aggravate	careless
caliber	condition	casualty
communicative	curable	cautious
disinterested	development	dangerous
expectation	diagnosis	disaster
guidance	fatigue	harmful
imperative	fitness	hastily
inadequate	hygiene	hazardous
incomplete	lethargic	injurious
incomprehensible	medication	insensible
inefficient	melancholy	precarious
inconclusive	nutritious	precaution
inconsistent	observation	protection
indifferent	recuperation	risky
inefficient	restless	vulnerable
insufficient	sensitive	
motivational	severe	
neglectful	symptoms	
participation	vigorous	
potential	well being	
preoccupied		
prerequisite		
priority		
privilege		
procrastination		
productive		
progressive		
quality		
unsatisfactory		

Notes:

_____

_____

_____

_____

_____

_____

_____

_____

_____

_____

_____

_____

_____

_____

_____

_____

_____

_____

_____

_____

_____

_____

Notes:

A NOTE HOME TO PARENTS

Student _____ **Date** _____

Dear Parents:

_____

Teacher's Signature

Parent's Reply

☐ Please comment, and have your child return this lower section to the teacher.

☐ No need to respond.

_____

_____

_____

_____

_____

Parent's Signature _____ **Date** _____

A NOTE HOME TO PARENTS

Student _____ Date _____

Dear Parents:

_____

_____

_____

Teacher's Signature _____

Parent's Reply

☐ Please comment and have your child return this lower section to the teacher.

☐ No need to respond.

_____

_____

_____

_____

Parent's Signature _____ Date _____

A NOTE HOME TO PARENTS

Student _____ Date _____

Dear Parents: _____

_____

_____

_____

_____

_____

_____

_____

_____

_____ Teacher's Signature

- -

Parent's Reply

☐ Please comment, and have your child return this lower section to the teacher.

☐ No need to respond.

_____

☐ Reply received _____ (date)
☐ No reply received.
☐ _____

☐ Second note sent home.
☐ Telephone call made _____ (date)
☐ Home visit _____ (date)

Teacher's Comment _____

_____

Teacher's Follow-Up _____

_____

A NOTE HOME TO
PARENTS

Student _____ **Date** _____

Dear Parents:

_____
Teacher's Signature

- - -

Parent's Reply

☐ Please comment, and have your child return this lower section to the teacher.

☐ No need to respond.

_____

_____

_____

_____

Parent's Signature _____ **Date** _____

© Teacher's Friend

A NOTE HOME TO
PARENTS

Student _____ Date _____

Dear Parents:

Teacher's Signature _____

Parents Reply

☐ Please comment, and have your child return this lower section to the teacher.

☐ No need to respond.

Parent's Signature _____ Date _____

A NOTE HOME TO
PARENTS

Student _____ Date _____

Dear Parents: _____

_____

_____

_____

_____

_____

_____

_____

_____

_____

Teacher's Signature

Parent's Reply

☐ Please comment, and have your child return this lower section to the teacher.

☐ No need to respond.

☐ Reply received _____ (date)
☐ No reply received.
☐ _____

☐ Second note sent home.
☐ Telephone call made _____ (date)
☐ Home visit _____ (date)

Teacher's Comment _____

_____

Teacher's Follow-Up _____

_____

A NOTE HOME TO PARENTS

Student _____ Date _____

Dear Parents,

_____

_____

_____

_____

_____

_____

_____

_____

_____

_____
Teacher's Signature

Parent's Reply

☐ Please comment, and have your child
return this lower section to the teacher.

☐ No need to respond.

☐ Reply received _____ (date)
☐ No reply received
☐ _____

☐ Second note sent home
☐ Telephone call made _____ (date)
☐ Home visit _____ (date)

Teacher's Comment _____

Teacher's Follow-Up _____

_____

A NOTE HOME TO
PARENTS

Student _____ Date _____

Dear Parents:

_____ _____
                                  Teacher's Signature

Parent's Reply   ☐ Please comment, and have your child return this lower section to the teacher.

☐ No need to respond.

_____

_____

_____

_____

_____

Parent's Signature _____ **Date** _____

A NOTE HOME TO PARENTS

Student _____ Date _____

Dear Parents,

_____

Teacher's Signature

Parent's Reply

☐ Please comment and have your child return this lower section to the teacher.

☐ No need to respond.

Parent's Signature _____ Date _____

A NOTE HOME TO PARENTS

Student _____   Date _____

Dear Parents: _____

_____

_____

_____

_____

_____

_____

_____

_____

_____   _____

Teacher's Signature

Parent's Reply

☐ Please comment, and have your child return this lower section to the teacher.

☐ No need to respond.

☐ Reply received _____ (date)
☐ No reply received.
☐ _____

☐ Second note sent home.
☐ Telephone call made _____ (date)
☐ Home visit _____ (date)

Teacher's Comment _____

_____

Teacher's Follow-Up _____

_____

A NOTE HOME TO PARENTS

Student _____ Date _____

Dear Parents:

_____

_____

_____

_____

_____

_____

_____

_____

_____

Teacher's Signature _____

☐ Please comment, and have your child return this lower section to the teacher.

☐ No need to respond.

Parent's Reply

☐ Reply received _____ (date)

☐ No reply received

☐ _____

Teacher's Comment _____

_____

Teacher's Follow-Up _____

_____

☐ Second note sent home

☐ Telephone call made _____ (date)

☐ Home visit _____ (date)

A NOTE HOME TO
PARENTS

Student _____ **Date** _____

Dear Parents:

_____ **Teacher's Signature**

- -

Parent's Reply

☐ Please comment, and have your child return this lower section to the teacher.

☐ No need to respond.

_____

_____

_____

_____

_____

Parent's Signature _____ **Date** _____

A NOTE HOME TO
PARENTS

Student

Date

Dear Parents:

Teacher's Signature

Parent's
Reply

☐ Please comment, and have your child
return this lower section to the teacher.

☐ No need to respond.

Parent's Signature

Date

A NOTE HOME TO PARENTS

Student _____ Date _____

Dear Parents: _____

_____

_____

_____

_____

_____

_____

_____

_____

_____
Teacher's Signature

- -

Parent's Reply

☐ Please comment, and have your child return this lower section to the teacher.

☐ No need to respond.

_____

☐ Reply received _____ (date)
☐ No reply received.
☐ _____

☐ Second note sent home.
☐ Telephone call made _____ (date)
☐ Home visit _____ (date)

Teacher's Comment _____

_____

Teacher's Follow-Up _____

_____

A NOTE HOME TO PARENTS

Student _____ Date _____

Dear Parents:

_____

_____

_____

_____

_____

_____

_____

_____

_____

_____

Teacher's Signature _____

Parent's Reply

☐ Please comment and have your child return this lower section to the teacher

☐ No need to respond.

Teacher's Comment

☐ Reply received _____ (date)
☐ No reply received.
☐

☐ Second note sent home.
☐ Telephone call made _____ (date)
☐ Home visit _____ (date)

Teacher's Follow-Up

_____

_____

A NOTE HOME TO
PARENTS

Student _____   **Date** _____

Dear Parents:

_____   **Teacher's Signature**

- -

Parent's Reply

☐ Please comment, and have your child return this lower section to the teacher.

☐ No need to respond.

Parent's Signature _____   **Date** _____

A NOTE HOME TO PARENTS

Student _____ Date _____

Dear Parents,

_____

Teacher's Signature _____

Parent's Reply

☐ Please comment and have your child return this lower section to the teacher.

☐ No need to respond.

Parent's Signature _____ Date _____

A NOTE HOME TO PARENTS

Student _____   Date _____

Dear Parents: _____

_____

_____

_____

_____

_____

_____

_____

_____

_____

_____   **Teacher's Signature**

- -

Parent's Reply

☐ Please comment, and have your child return this lower section to the teacher.

☐ No need to respond.

☐ Reply received _____ (date)   ☐ Second note sent home.

☐ No reply received.   ☐ Telephone call made _____ (date)

☐ _____   ☐ Home visit _____ (date)

Teacher's Comment _____

_____

Teacher's Follow-Up _____

_____

A NOTE HOME TO
PARENTS

A NOTE HOME TO PARENTS

Student _____ Date _____

Dear Parents:

_____

_____

_____

_____

_____

_____

_____

_____

_____

Teacher's Signature _____

Parent's Reply

☐ Please comment, and have your child return this lower section to the teacher.

☐ No need to respond.

☐ Reply received _____ (date)
☐ No reply received
☐

☐ Second note sent home
☐ Telephone call made _____ (date)
☐ Home visit _____ (date)

Teacher's Comment _____

Teacher's Follow-Up _____

_____

A NOTE HOME TO
PARENTS

Student _____ **Date** _____

Dear Parents:

_____ **Teacher's Signature**

- -

Parent's Reply

☐ Please comment, and have your child return this lower section to the teacher.

☐ No need to respond.

_____

_____

_____

_____

Parent's Signature _____ **Date** _____

A NOTE HOME TO PARENTS

Student

Date

Dear Parents:

Teacher's Signature

Parent's Reply

☐ Please comment, and have your child return this lower section to the teacher.

☐ No need to respond.

Parent's Signature

Date

A NOTE HOME TO PARENTS

Student _____ Date _____

Dear Parents: _____

_____

_____

_____

_____

_____

_____

_____

_____

_____   Teacher's Signature

- -

Parent's Reply

☐ Please comment, and have your child return this lower section to the teacher.

☐ No need to respond.

_____

☐ Reply received _____ (date)
☐ No reply received.
☐ _____

☐ Second note sent home.
☐ Telephone call made _____ (date)
☐ Home visit _____ (date)

Teacher's Comment _____

_____

Teacher's Follow-Up _____

_____

A NOTE HOME TO PARENTS

Student _____

Date _____

Dear Parents:

_____

_____

_____

_____

_____

_____

_____

_____

Teacher's Signature _____

Parent's Reply

☐ Please comment, and have your child return this lower section to the teacher.

☐ No need to respond

☐ Reply received _____ (date)

☐ No reply received.

☐ _____

☐ Second note sent home _____

☐ Telephone call made _____ (date)

☐ Home visit _____ (date)

Teacher's Comment _____

_____

Teacher's Follow-Up _____

_____

© Teacher's Friend

A NOTE HOME TO
PARENTS

Student _____ **Date** _____

Dear Parents:

_____

Teacher's Signature

- -

Parent's Reply

☐ Please comment, and have your child return this lower section to the teacher.

☐ No need to respond.

_____

Parent's Signature _____ **Date** _____

A NOTE HOME TO PARENTS

Student _____ Date _____

Dear Parents,

Teacher's Signature _____

Parent's Reply

☐ Please comment, and have your child return this lower section to the teacher.

☐ No need to respond.

Parent's Signature _____ Date _____

A NOTE HOME TO
PARENTS

Student _____ Date _____

Dear Parents: _____

_____

_____

_____

_____

_____

_____

_____

_____

_____ **Teacher's Signature**

Parent's Reply

☐ Please comment, and have your child return this lower section to the teacher.

☐ No need to respond.

_____

☐ Reply received _____ (date)   ☐ Second note sent home.

☐ No reply received.   ☐ Telephone call made _____ (date)

☐   ☐ Home visit _____ (date)

Teacher's Comment _____

_____

Teacher's Follow-Up _____

_____

A NOTE HOME TO PARENTS

Student _____

Date _____

Dear Parents:

_____

_____

_____

_____

_____

_____

_____

_____

Teacher's Signature _____

Parent's Reply

☐ Please comment, and have your child return this lower section to the teacher.

☐ No need to respond.

☐ Reply received _____ (date)

☐ No reply received

☐ Second note sent home.

☐ Telephone call made _____ (date)

☐ Home visit _____ (date)

Teacher's Comment _____

Teacher's Follow-Up _____

A NOTE HOME TO PARENTS

Student _____   **Date** _____

Dear Parents:

_____
Teacher's Signature

- -

Parent's Reply

☐ Please comment, and have your child return this lower section to the teacher.

☐ No need to respond.

_____
_____
_____
_____

Parent's Signature _____   **Date** _____

© Teacher's Friend

A NOTE HOME TO PARENTS

Student _____ Date _____

Dear Parents:

_____

Teacher's Signature

Parent's Reply

☐ Please comment and have your child return this lower section to the teacher.

☐ No need to respond.

Parent's Signature _____ Date _____

A NOTE HOME TO
PARENTS

Student _____ **Date** _____

Dear Parents: _____

_____

_____

_____

_____

_____

_____

_____

_____

_____ **Teacher's Signature**

- -

Parent's Reply

☐ Please comment, and have your child return this lower section to the teacher.

☐ No need to respond.

_____

☐ Reply received _____ (date)   ☐ Second note sent home.

☐ No reply received.   ☐ Telephone call made _____ (date)

☐ _____   ☐ Home visit _____ (date)

Teacher's Comment _____

_____

Teacher's Follow-Up _____

_____

A NOTE HOME TO PARENTS

Student _____

Date _____

Dear Parents _____

_____

_____

_____

_____

_____

_____

_____

Teacher's Signature _____

Parent's Reply

☐ Please comment and have your child return this lower section to the teacher.

☐ No need to respond.

_____

☐ Reply received _____ (date)

☐ No reply received.

☐ Second note sent home.

☐ Telephone call made _____ (date)

☐ Home visit _____ (date)

Teacher's Comment _____

_____

Teacher's Follow-Up _____

_____

© Teacher's Friend

A NOTE HOME TO
PARENTS

Student _____ **Date** _____

Dear Parents:

_____
Teacher's Signature

Parent's Reply ☐ Please comment, and have your child return this lower section to the teacher.

☐ No need to respond.

_____
_____
_____
_____
_____

Parent's Signature _____ **Date** _____

A NOTE HOME TO PARENTS

Student _____ Date _____

Dear Parents,

Teacher's Signature _____

Parent's Reply

☐ Please comment, and have your child
   return this lower section to his/her class.

☐ No need to respond.

Parent's Signature _____ Date _____

A NOTE HOME TO PARENTS

Student _____ **Date** _____

Dear Parents: _____

_____

_____

_____

_____

_____

_____

_____

_____

_____   **Teacher's Signature**

Parent's Reply

☐ Please comment, and have your child return this lower section to the teacher.

☐ No need to respond.

_____

☐ Reply received _____ (date)
☐ No reply received.
☐ _____

☐ Second note sent home.
☐ Telephone call made _____ (date)
☐ Home visit _____ (date)

Teacher's Comment _____

_____

Teacher's Follow-Up _____

_____

A NOTE HOME TO PARENTS

Student _____   Date _____

Dear Parents:

_____

_____

_____

_____

_____

_____

_____

_____

Teacher's Signature _____

Parent's Reply

☐ Please comment, and have your child return this lower section to the teacher.

☐ No need to respond.

☐ Reply received _____ (date)

☐ No reply received.

☐ _____

☐ Second note sent home.

☐ Telephone call made _____ (date)

☐ Home visit _____ (date)

Teacher's Comment _____

Teacher's Follow-Up _____

A NOTE HOME TO
PARENTS

Student _____

Date _____

Dear Parents:

_____

Teacher's Signature

- -

Parent's Reply

☐ Please comment, and have your child return this lower section to the teacher.

☐ No need to respond.

_____

_____

_____

_____

_____

Parent's Signature _____

Date _____

A NOTE HOME TO PARENTS

Student

Date

Dear Parents:

Teacher's Signature

Parent's Reply

☐ Please comment and have your child return this lower section to the teacher.

☐ No need to respond.

Parent's Signature

Date

A NOTE HOME TO
PARENTS

Student _____ Date _____

Dear Parents: _____

_____

_____

_____

_____

_____

_____

_____

_____

_____

_____ **Teacher's Signature**

Parent's Reply

☐ Please comment, and have your child return this lower section to the teacher.

☐ No need to respond.

_____

☐ Reply received _____ (date)

☐ No reply received.

☐ _____

☐ Second note sent home.

☐ Telephone call made _____ (date)

☐ Home visit _____ (date)

Teacher's Comment _____

_____

Teacher's Follow-Up _____

_____

A NOTE HOME TO PARENTS

Student _____ Date _____

Dear Parents:

_____

_____

_____

_____

_____

_____

_____

_____

Teacher's Signature _____

Parent's Reply

☐ Please comment, and have your child
   return this lower section to the teacher.

☐ No need to respond.

☐ Reply received _____ (date)

☐ No reply received.

☐ Second note sent home.

☐ Telephone call made. _____ (date)

☐ Home visit _____ (date)

Teacher's Comment _____

_____

Teacher's Follow-Up _____

_____

© Teacher's Friend

A NOTE HOME TO
PARENTS

Student _____

Date _____

Dear Parents:

_____

Teacher's Signature

- -

Parent's Reply

☐ Please comment, and have your child return this lower section to the teacher.

☐ No need to respond.

_____

_____

_____

_____

_____

Parent's Signature

Date

A NOTE HOME TO PARENTS

Student _____ Date _____

Dear Parents:

_____ Teacher's Signature

Parent's Reply

☐ Please comment, and have your child return this lower section to the teacher.

☐ No, need to respond.

Parent's Signature _____ Date _____

A NOTE HOME TO PARENTS

Student _____ Date _____

Dear Parents: _____

_____

_____

_____

_____

_____

_____

_____

_____

_____

Teacher's Signature

Parent's Reply

☐ Please comment, and have your child return this lower section to the teacher.

☐ No need to respond.

☐ Reply received _____ (date)

☐ No reply received.

☐ _____

☐ Second note sent home.

☐ Telephone call made _____ (date)

☐ Home visit _____ (date)

Teacher's Comment _____

_____

Teacher's Follow-Up _____

_____

A NOTE HOME TO PARENTS

Student: _____

Date _____

Dear Parents: _____

_____

_____

_____

_____

_____

_____

_____

Teacher's Signature _____

Parent's Reply

☐ Please comment, and have your child return this lower section to the teacher.

☐ No need to respond.

☐ Reply received _____ (date)

☐ No reply received.

☐

☐ Second note sent home _____

☐ Telephone call made _____ (date)

☐ Home visit _____ (date)

Teacher's Comment _____

_____

Teacher's Follow-Up _____

_____

© Teacher's Friend

A NOTE HOME TO
PARENTS

Student _____ **Date** _____

Dear Parents:

_____

Teacher's Signature

- -

Parent's Reply

☐ Please comment, and have your child return this lower section to the teacher.

☐ No need to respond.

_____

_____

_____

_____

_____

Parent's Signature _____ **Date** _____

A NOTE HOME TO PARENTS

Student _____ Date _____

Dear Parents:

Teacher's Signature _____

Parent's Reply

☐ Please comment, and have your child return this lower section to me tomorrow.

☐ No need to respond.

Parent's Signature _____ Date _____

A NOTE HOME TO
PARENTS

Student _____ Date _____

Dear Parents: _____

_____

_____

_____

_____

_____

_____

_____

_____

_____

Teacher's Signature

- -

Parent's Reply

☐ Please comment, and have your child return this lower section to the teacher.

☐ No need to respond.

_____

☐ Reply received _____ (date)
☐ No reply received.
☐ _____

☐ Second note sent home.
☐ Telephone call made _____ (date)
☐ Home visit _____ (date)

Teacher's Comment _____

_____

Teacher's Follow-Up _____

_____

A NOTE HOME TO
PARENTS

Student _____

Date _____

Dear Parents:

_____

_____

_____

_____

_____

_____

_____

_____

Teacher's Signature _____

Parent's Reply

☐ Please comment, and have your child
return this lower section to the teacher.

☐ No need to respond.

_____

☐ Reply received _____ (date)

☐ No reply received _____

☐ _____

☐ Second note sent home _____

☐ Telephone call made _____ (date)

☐ Home visit _____ (date)

Teacher's Comment _____

Teacher's Follow-Up _____

A NOTE HOME TO
PARENTS

Student _____

Date _____

Dear Parents:

_____

Teacher's Signature

- -

Parent's Reply

☐ Please comment, and have your child return this lower section to the teacher.

☐ No need to respond.

_____

Parent's Signature

Date

A NOTE HOME TO PARENTS

Student _____ Date _____

Dear Parents:

_____

Teacher's Signature

Parent's Reply

□ Please comment, and have your child return this lower section to the teacher.

□ No need to respond

Parent's Signature _____ Date _____

A NOTE HOME TO
PARENTS

Student _____   **Date** _____

Dear Parents: _____

_____

_____

_____

_____

_____

_____

_____

_____

_____

Teacher's Signature

Parent's Reply

☐ Please comment, and have your child return this lower section to the teacher.

☐ No need to respond.

☐ Reply received _____ (date)
☐ No reply received.
☐ _____

☐ Second note sent home.
☐ Telephone call made _____ (date)
☐ Home visit _____ (date)

Teacher's Comment _____

_____

Teacher's Follow-Up _____

_____

Student _____

Date _____

Dear Parents,

_____

_____

_____

_____

_____

_____

_____

_____

Teacher's Signature _____

Parent's Reply

☐ Please comfort and have your child
   return this lower section to the teacher.

☐ No need to respond.

☐ Reply received _____ (date)	☐ Second note sent home
☐ No reply received.	☐ Telephone call made _____ (date)
☐ _____	☐ Home visit _____ (date)

Teacher's Comments _____

_____

Teacher's Follow-Up _____

_____

_____

A NOTE HOME TO
PARENTS

Student _____

Date _____

Dear Parents:

_____

Teacher's Signature

Parent's Reply

☐ Please comment, and have your child return this lower section to the teacher.

☐ No need to respond.

_____
_____
_____
_____
_____

Parent's Signature _____

Date _____

A NOTE HOME TO
PARENTS

Student _____ Date _____

Dear Parents,

_____
Teacher's Signature

Parent's Reply

☐ Please comment and have your child return this lower section to the teacher.

☐ No need to respond.

_____
Parent's Signature _____ Date _____

A NOTE HOME TO
PARENTS

Student _____   Date

Dear Parents: _____

_____

_____

_____

_____

_____

_____

_____

_____

_____

_____   Teacher's Signature

Parent's Reply

☐ Please comment, and have your child return this lower section to the teacher.

☐ No need to respond.

☐ Reply received _____ (date)
☐ No reply received.
☐ _____

☐ Second note sent home.
☐ Telephone call made _____ (date)
☐ Home visit _____ (date)

Teacher's Comment _____

_____

Teacher's Follow-Up _____

_____

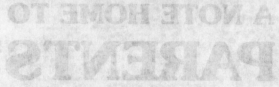

A NOTE HOME TO PARENTS

Student _____ Date _____

Dear Parents:

_____

_____

_____

_____

_____

_____

_____

_____

_____

Teacher's Signature _____

Parent's Reply

☐ Please comment and have your child
return this lower section to the teacher.

☐ No need to respond

☐ Reply received _____ (date)

☐ No reply received.

☐

☐ Second note sent home

☐ Telephone call made _____ (date)

☐ Home visit _____ (date)

Teacher's Comment _____

Teacher's Follow-Up _____

A NOTE HOME TO
PARENTS

_____

Student

Date

Dear Parents:

_____

Teacher's Signature

- -

Parent's Reply

☐ Please comment, and have your child return this lower section to the teacher.

☐ No need to respond.

_____

Parent's Signature

Date

A NOTE HOME TO PARENTS

Student _____ Date _____

Dear Parents:

_____

Teacher's Signature _____

Parent's Reply

☐ Please comment, and have your child return this later section to the teacher.

☐ No need to respond.

_____
_____
_____
_____

Parent's Signature _____ Date _____

A NOTE HOME TO PARENTS

Student _____   Date _____

Dear Parents: _____

_____

_____

_____

_____

_____

_____

_____

_____

_____   _____

Teacher's Signature

- -

Parent's Reply

☐ Please comment, and have your child return this lower section to the teacher.

☐ No need to respond.

_____

☐ Reply received _____ (date)

☐ No reply received.

☐ _____

☐ Second note sent home.

☐ Telephone call made _____ (date)

☐ Home visit _____ (date)

Teacher's Comment _____

_____

Teacher's Follow-Up _____

_____

© Teacher's Friend

A NOTE HOME TO PARENTS

Student _____

Date _____

Dear Parents:

_____

_____

_____

_____

_____

_____

Teacher's Signature _____

Parent's Reply

☐ Please comment and have your child return this lower section to me/teacher.

☐ No need to respond

☐ Reply received _____ (date)

☐ No reply received

☐ Second note sent home

☐ Telephone call made _____ (date)

☐ Home visit _____ (date)

Teacher's Comment _____

Teacher's Follow-Up _____

© Teacher Created

A NOTE HOME TO PARENTS

_____   _____
Student   **Date**

Dear Parents:

_____
Teacher's Signature

- -

Parent's Reply

☐ Please comment, and have your child return this lower section to the teacher.

☐ No need to respond.

_____   _____
Parent's Signature   **Date**

A NOTE HOME TO PARENTS

Student _____ Date _____

Dear Parents:

_____

Teacher's Signature

Parent's Reply

☐ Please comment and have your child return this lower section to the teacher.

☐ No need to respond.

Parent's Signature _____ Date _____

A NOTE HOME TO
PARENTS

Student _____ **Date** _____

Dear Parents: _____

_____

_____

_____

_____

_____

_____

_____

_____

_____ **Teacher's Signature**

- -

Parent's Reply

☐ Please comment, and have your child return this lower section to the teacher.

☐ No need to respond.

_____

☐ Reply received _____ (date)   ☐ Second note sent home.

☐ No reply received.   ☐ Telephone call made _____ (date)

☐ _____   ☐ Home visit _____ (date)

Teacher's Comment _____

_____

Teacher's Follow-Up _____

_____

A NOTE HOME TO PARENTS

Student _____ Date _____

Dear Parents:

_____

_____

_____

_____

_____

_____

_____

_____

_____

Teacher's Signature _____

Parent's Reply

☐ Please comment, and have your child
   return his lower section to the teacher.

☐ No need to respond.

☐ Reply received _____ (date)

☐ No reply received.

☐ _____

☐ Second note sent home
☐ Telephone call made _____ (date)
☐ Home visit _____ (date)

Teacher's Comment _____

Teacher's Follow-Up _____

A NOTE HOME TO
PARENTS

Student _____ **Date** _____

Dear Parents:

_____

Teacher's Signature

- -

Parent's Reply

☐ Please comment, and have your child return this lower section to the teacher.

☐ No need to respond.

_____

_____

_____

_____

_____

Parent's Signature _____ **Date** _____

A NOTE HOME TO PARENTS

Student: _____

Date _____

Dear Parents:

_____

Teacher's Signature

Parent's Reply

☐ Please comment, and have your child return this lower section to the teacher.

☐ No need to respond.

_____

_____

_____

_____

Parent's Signature _____ Date _____

A NOTE HOME TO PARENTS

Student _____   Date _____

Dear Parents: _____

_____

_____

_____

_____

_____

_____

_____

_____

_____   **Teacher's Signature**

Parent's Reply

☐ Please comment, and have your child return this lower section to the teacher.

☐ No need to respond.

☐ Reply received _____ (date)
☐ No reply received.
☐ _____

☐ Second note sent home.
☐ Telephone call made _____ (date)
☐ Home visit _____ (date)

Teacher's Comment _____

_____

Teacher's Follow-Up _____

_____

A NOTE HOME TO PARENTS

Student _____

Date _____

Dear Parents:

_____

_____

_____

_____

_____

_____

_____

Teacher's Signature _____

Parent's Reply

☐ Please comment, and have your child return this lower section to the teacher.

☐ No need to respond.

☐ Reply received _____ (date)

☐ No reply received.

☐ _____

☐ Second note sent home

☐ Telephone call made _____ (date)

☐ Home visit _____ (date)

Teacher's Comment _____

Teacher's Follow-Up _____

A NOTE HOME TO
PARENTS

Student _____   Date _____

Dear Parents:

_____   Teacher's Signature

- -

Parent's Reply

☐ Please comment, and have your child return this lower section to the teacher.

☐ No need to respond.

_____

_____

_____

_____

_____

Parent's Signature _____   Date _____

A NOTE HOME TO PARENTS

Student _____ Date _____

Dear Parents:

_____

Teacher's Signature _____

Parent's Reply

☐ Please comment, and I have your child
return this lower section to the teacher.

☐ No need to respond.

Parent's Signature _____ Date _____

A NOTE HOME TO PARENTS

Student _____   **Date** _____

Dear Parents: _____

_____

_____

_____

_____

_____

_____

_____

_____

_____

Teacher's Signature

Parent's Reply

☐ Please comment, and have your child return this lower section to the teacher.

☐ No need to respond.

☐ Reply received _____ (date)
☐ No reply received.
☐ _____

☐ Second note sent home.
☐ Telephone call made _____ (date)
☐ Home visit _____ (date)

Teacher's Comment _____

_____

Teacher's Follow-Up _____

_____

A NOTE HOME TO PARENTS

Student _____ Date _____

Dear Parents:

_____

_____

_____

_____

_____

_____

Teacher's Signature _____

Parent's Reply

☐ Please comment, and have your child
   return this lower section to the teacher.

☐ No need to respond.

☐ Reply received _____ (date)   ☐ Second note sent home

☐ No reply received   ☐ Telephone call made _____ (date)

☐   ☐ Home visit _____ (date)

Teacher's Comment _____

Teacher's Follow-Up _____

A NOTE HOME TO
PARENTS

Student _____ **Date** _____

Dear Parents:

_____

Teacher's Signature _____

- -

Parent's Reply

☐ Please comment, and have your child return this lower section to the teacher.

☐ No need to respond.

_____

_____

_____

_____

_____

Parent's Signature _____ **Date** _____

A NOTE HOME TO PARENTS

Student _____   Date _____

Dear Parents:

_____

_____

_____

_____

_____

_____

_____

_____

_____

_____

_____

Teacher's Signature _____

Parent's Reply

☐ Please comment, and have your child
return this lower section to the teacher.

☐ No need to respond.

_____

_____

_____

_____

_____

_____

Parent's Signature _____   Date _____

A NOTE HOME TO
PARENTS

Student _____ **Date** _____

Dear Parents: _____

_____

_____

_____

_____

_____

_____

_____

_____

_____ **Teacher's Signature**

Parent's Reply

☐ Please comment, and have your child return this lower section to the teacher.

☐ No need to respond.

_____

☐ Reply received _____ (date)
☐ No reply received.
☐ _____

☐ Second note sent home.
☐ Telephone call made _____ (date)
☐ Home visit _____ (date)

Teacher's Comment _____

_____

Teacher's Follow-Up _____

_____

A NOTE HOME TO PARENTS

Student _____ Date _____

Dear Parents:

_____

_____

_____

_____

_____

_____

_____

Teacher's Signature _____

Parent's Reply

☐ Please comment and have your child return this lower section to the teacher.

☐ No need to respond.

_____

Teacher's Comment _____

☐ Reply received _____ (date)
☐ No reply received
☐

☐ Second note sent home
☐ Telephone called _____ (date)
☐ Home visit _____ (date)

_____

Teacher's Follow-Up _____

_____

A NOTE HOME TO
PARENTS

Student _____ **Date** _____

Dear Parents:

_____ **Teacher's Signature**

- -

Parent's Reply

☐ Please comment, and have your child return this lower section to the teacher.

☐ No need to respond.

_____

_____

_____

_____

_____

Parent's Signature _____ **Date** _____

A NOTE HOME TO PARENTS

Student _____ Date _____

Dear Parents: _____

_____

_____

_____

_____

_____

_____

_____

_____

_____

_____ _____

Teacher's Signature

- -

Parent's Reply

☐ Please comment, and have your child return this lower section to the teacher.

☐ No need to respond.

☐ Reply received _____ (date)

☐ No reply received.

☐ _____

☐ Second note sent home.

☐ Telephone call made _____ (date)

☐ Home visit _____ (date)

Teacher's Comment _____

_____

Teacher's Follow-Up _____

_____

A NOTE HOME TO PARENTS

Student _____ Date _____

Dear Parents:

_____

_____

_____

_____

_____

_____

_____

_____
Teacher's Signature

Parent's Reply

☐ Please comment and have your child return this lower section to the teacher.

☐ No need to respond.

☐ Reply received _____ (date)
☐ No reply received.
☐

☐ Second note sent home
☐ Telephone call made _____
☐ Home visit _____

Teacher's Comment _____

Teacher's Follow-Up _____

A NOTE HOME TO
PARENTS

Student _____ **Date** _____

Dear Parents:

_____ _____

Teacher's Signature

- -

Parent's Reply

☐ Please comment, and have your child return this lower section to the teacher.

☐ No need to respond.

_____

_____

_____

_____

_____

Parent's Signature _____ **Date** _____

A NOTE HOME TO PARENTS

Student _____ Date _____

Dear Parents:

Teacher's Signature _____

Parent's Reply

[ ] Please comment, and have your child return this lower section to the teacher.

[ ] No need to respond.

Parent's Signature _____ Date _____

A NOTE HOME TO
PARENTS

Student _____   Date _____

Dear Parents: _____

_____

_____

_____

_____

_____

_____

_____

_____

_____

Teacher's Signature

Parent's Reply

☐ Please comment, and have your child
   return this lower section to the teacher.

☐ No need to respond.

☐ Reply received _____ (date)

☐ No reply received.

☐ _____

☐ Second note sent home.

☐ Telephone call made _____ (date)

☐ Home visit _____ (date)

Teacher's Comment _____

_____

Teacher's Follow-Up _____

_____

A NOTE HOME TO PARENTS

Student _____ Date _____

Dear Parents:

_____

_____

_____

_____

_____

_____

_____

_____

_____

Teacher's Signature _____

☐ Please comment, and have your child
   return this lower section to the teacher.

☐ No need to respond.

Parent's Reply

☐ Reply received _____ (date)

☐ No reply received.

☐ _____

Teacher's Comment _____

☐ Second note sent home.

☐ Telephone call made _____ (date)

☐ Home visit _____ (date)

Teacher's Follow-Up _____

_____

_____

A NOTE HOME TO
PARENTS

Student _____ **Date** _____

Dear Parents:

_____ **Teacher's Signature**

Parent's Reply ☐ Please comment, and have your child return this lower section to the teacher.

☐ No need to respond.

_____

_____

_____

_____

_____

Parent's Signature _____ **Date** _____

A NOTE HOME TO PARENTS

Student: _____

Date: _____

Dear Parents,

_____

Teacher's Signature: _____

Parent's Reply

☐ Please comment and have your child return this lower section to the teacher.

☐ No need to respond.

_____

Parent's Signature: _____   Date: _____

A NOTE HOME TO
PARENTS

Student _____   **Date** _____

Dear Parents: _____

_____

_____

_____

_____

_____

_____

_____

_____

_____

_____   **Teacher's Signature**

- -

Parent's Reply

☐ Please comment, and have your child return this lower section to the teacher.

☐ No need to respond.

☐ Reply received _____ (date)
☐ No reply received.
☐ _____

☐ Second note sent home.
☐ Telephone call made _____ (date)
☐ Home visit _____ (date)

Teacher's Comment _____

_____

Teacher's Follow-Up _____

_____

A NOTE HOME TO PARENTS

Student _____

Date _____

Dear Parents, _____

_____

_____

_____

_____

_____

_____

_____

Teacher's Signature _____

Parent's Reply

☐ Please comment, and have your child return this lower section to the teacher

☐ No need to respond.

_____

☐ Reply received _____ (date)

☐ No reply received

☐ _____

☐ Second note sent home _____

☐ Telephone call made _____ (date)

☐ Home visit _____ (date)

Teacher's Comment _____

_____

Teacher's Follow-Up _____

_____

A NOTE HOME TO PARENTS

Student _____ **Date** _____

Dear Parents:

_____ **Teacher's Signature**

- -

Parent's Reply

☐ Please comment, and have your child return this lower section to the teacher.

☐ No need to respond.

_____

_____

_____

_____

_____

_____

Parent's Signature _____ **Date** _____

Student: _____

Date _____

Dear Parents:

_____

_____

_____

Teacher's Signature

Parent's
Reply

☐ Please comment, and have your child
return this lower section to the teacher.

☐ No need to respond

A NOTE HOME TO
PARENTS

Parent's Signature _____   Date _____

A NOTE HOME TO
PARENTS

Student _____   Date _____

Dear Parents: _____

_____

_____

_____

_____

_____

_____

_____

_____

_____

_____   Teacher's Signature

- -

Parent's Reply

☐ Please comment, and have your child return this lower section to the teacher.

☐ No need to respond.

☐ Reply received _____ (date)

☐ No reply received.

☐ _____

☐ Second note sent home.

☐ Telephone call made _____ (date)

☐ Home visit _____ (date)

Teacher's Comment _____

_____

Teacher's Follow-Up _____

_____

A NOTE HOME TO
PARENTS

Student _____ Date _____

Dear Parents:

_____

_____

_____

_____

_____

_____

_____

_____

Teacher's Signature _____

Parent's Reply

☐ Please comment, and have your child
    return this lower section to the teacher.

☐ No, need to reschedule.

☐ Reply received _____ (date)

☐ No reply received

☐ _____

☐ Second note sent home.

☐ Telephone call made _____ (date)

☐ Home visit _____ (date)

Teacher's Comment _____

Teacher's Follow-Up _____

© Teacher Friend

A NOTE HOME TO
PARENTS

_____ _____
Student   **Date**

Dear Parents:

_____ _____
                           Teacher's Signature

- -

Parent's Reply

☐ Please comment, and have your child return this lower section to the teacher.

☐ No need to respond.

_____

_____

_____

_____

_____

_____ _____
Parent's Signature   **Date**

A NOTE HOME TO PARENTS

Student: _____ Date _____

Dear Parents:

_____

Teacher's Signature

☐ **Parent's Reply** Please comment, and have your child return this lower section to the teacher.

☐ No need to respond.

Parent's Signature _____ Date _____

A NOTE HOME TO
PARENTS

Student _____   **Date** _____

Dear Parents: _____

_____

_____

_____

_____

_____

_____

_____

_____

Teacher's Signature

- -

Parent's Reply

☐ Please comment, and have your child return this lower section to the teacher.

☐ No need to respond.

_____

☐ Reply received _____ (date)

☐ No reply received.

☐ _____

☐ Second note sent home.

☐ Telephone call made _____ (date)

☐ Home visit _____ (date)

Teacher's Comment _____

_____

Teacher's Follow-Up _____

_____

A NOTE HOME TO
PARENTS

Student _____ **Date** _____

Dear Parents:

_____

Teacher's Signature

- -

Parent's Reply

☐ Please comment, and have your child
return this lower section to the teacher.

☐ No need to respond.

_____

_____

_____

_____

_____

Parent's Signature _____ **Date** _____

A NOTE HOME TO PARENTS

Student _____ Date _____

Dear Parents:

Teacher's Signature _____

Parent's Reply

☐ Please comment and have your child return this lower section to the teacher.

☐ No need to respond.

Parent's Signature _____ Date _____

© Teacher Friendly

A NOTE HOME TO PARENTS

Student _____ **Date** _____

Dear Parents: _____

_____

_____

_____

_____

_____

_____

_____

_____

_____ **Teacher's Signature**

Parent's Reply

☐ Please comment, and have your child return this lower section to the teacher.

☐ No need to respond.

☐ Reply received _____ (date)   ☐ Second note sent home.
☐ No reply received.   ☐ Telephone call made _____ (date)
☐ _____   ☐ Home visit _____ (date)

Teacher's Comment _____

_____

Teacher's Follow-Up _____

_____

A NOTE HOME TO PARENTS

Student _____

Date _____

Dear Parents:

_____

_____

_____

_____

_____

_____

_____

Teacher's Signature _____

Parent's Reply

☐ Please comment and have your child
  return this lower section to the teacher.

☐ No need to respond.

_____

☐ Reply received _____ (date)

☐ No reply received.

☐ _____

☐ Second note sent home _____

☐ Telephone call made _____ (date)

☐ Home visit _____ (date)

Teacher's Comment _____

_____

Teacher's Follow-Up _____

_____

A NOTE HOME TO
PARENTS

Student _____   **Date** _____

Dear Parents:

_____   _____

Teacher's Signature

- -

Parent's Reply

☐ Please comment, and have your child return this lower section to the teacher.

☐ No need to respond.

_____

_____

_____

_____

_____

Parent's Signature _____   **Date** _____

A NOTE HOME TO PARENTS

Student

Date

Dear Parents,

Teacher's Signature

Parent's Reply

☐ Please comment, and I have your child return this lower section to the teacher.

☐ No need to respond.

Parent's Signature

Date

A NOTE HOME TO
PARENTS

Student _____   Date _____

Dear Parents: _____

_____

_____

_____

_____

_____

_____

_____

_____

_____

_____   _____
                                       Teacher's Signature

Parent's Reply

☐ Please comment, and have your child return this lower section to the teacher.

☐ No need to respond.

☐ Reply received _____ (date)   ☐ Second note sent home.

☐ No reply received.   ☐ Telephone call made _____ (date)

☐ _____   ☐ Home visit _____ (date)

Teacher's Comment _____

Teacher's Follow-Up _____

_____

A NOTE HOME TO PARENTS

Student _____ Date _____

Dear Parents:

_____

_____

_____

_____

_____

_____

_____

Teacher's Signature _____

Parent's Reply

☐ Please comment, and have your child return this lower section to the teacher.

☐ No need to respond.

☐ Reply received _____ (date)

☐ No reply received

☐ _____

Teacher's Comment _____

☐ Second note sent home

☐ Telephone call made _____ (time)

☐ Home visit _____ (date)

Teacher's Follow-Up _____

A NOTE HOME TO PARENTS

_____   _____
Student   **Date**

Dear Parents:

_____
Teacher's Signature

Parent's Reply   ☐ Please comment, and have your child return this lower section to the teacher.

☐ No need to respond.

_____   _____
Parent's Signature   **Date**

© Teacher's Friend

A NOTE HOME TO
PARENTS

Student _____   **Date** _____

Dear Parents: _____

_____

_____

_____

_____

_____

_____

_____

_____

_____

_____

Teacher's Signature

- -

Parent's Reply

☐ Please comment, and have your child return this lower section to the teacher.

☐ No need to respond.

☐ Reply received _____ (date)
☐ No reply received.
☐

☐ Second note sent home.
☐ Telephone call made _____ (date)
☐ Home visit _____ (date)

Teacher's Comment _____

_____

Teacher's Follow-Up _____

_____

© Teacher's Friend

A NOTE HOME TO PARENTS

Student _____ Date _____

Dear Parents:

_____

_____

_____

_____

_____

_____

_____

Teacher's Signature

Parent's Reply

☐ Please comment, and have your child return this lower section to the teacher.

☐ No need to respond.

☐ Reply received _____ (date)

☐ No reply received

☐

☐ Second note sent home.

☐ Telephone call made _____ (date)

☐ Home visit _____ (date)

Teacher's Comment _____

Teacher's Follow-Up _____

© Teacher Created

A NOTE HOME TO
PARENTS

_____   _____
Student   **Date**

Dear Parents:

_____

Teacher's Signature

Parent's Reply

☐ Please comment, and have your child return this lower section to the teacher.

☐ No need to respond.

_____

_____

_____

_____

_____

_____   _____
Parent's Signature   **Date**

A NOTE HOME TO PARENTS

Student _____

Date _____

Dear Parents:

_____ Teacher's Signature

Parent's Reply

☐ Please comment, and have your child return this lower section to the teacher.

☐ No need to respond.

_____ Parent's Signature

Date _____

A NOTE HOME TO PARENTS

Student _____ **Date** _____

Dear Parents: _____

_____

_____

_____

_____

_____

_____

_____

_____

_____ **Teacher's Signature**

- -

Parent's Reply

☐ Please comment, and have your child return this lower section to the teacher.

☐ No need to respond.

☐ Reply received _____ (date)
☐ No reply received.
☐ _____

☐ Second note sent home.
☐ Telephone call made _____ (date)
☐ Home visit _____ (date)

Teacher's Comment _____

_____

Teacher's Follow-Up _____

_____

© Teacher's Friend

A NOTE HOME TO PARENTS

Student _____ Date _____

Dear Parents,

_____

_____

_____

_____

_____

_____

_____

_____

Teacher's Signature _____

Parent's Reply

☐ Please comment and have your child
   return this lower section to the teacher.

☐ No need to respond.

☐ Reply received _____ (date)   ☐ Second note sent home.

☐ No reply received.   ☐ Telephone call made. _____ (date)

☐ _____   ☐ Home visit _____ (date)

Teacher's Comment _____

_____

Teacher's Follow-Up _____

A NOTE HOME TO
PARENTS

Student _____ **Date** _____

Dear Parents:

_____ **Teacher's Signature**

Parent's Reply

☐ Please comment, and have your child return this lower section to the teacher.

☐ No need to respond.

_____

_____

_____

_____

_____

Parent's Signature _____ **Date** _____

A NOTE HOME TO PARENTS

Student _____

Date _____

Dear Parents:

Teacher's Signature _____

Parents' Reply

☐ Please comment and have your child return this lower section to the teacher

☐ No need to respond

Parent's Signature _____

Date _____

A NOTE HOME TO
PARENTS

Student _____ **Date** _____

Dear Parents: _____
_____
_____
_____
_____
_____
_____
_____
_____
_____

_____
Teacher's Signature

Parent's Reply

☐ Please comment, and have your child return this lower section to the teacher.

☐ No need to respond.

_____

☐ Reply received _____ (date)
☐ No reply received.
☐ _____

☐ Second note sent home.
☐ Telephone call made _____ (date)
☐ Home visit _____ (date)

Teacher's Comment _____
_____

Teacher's Follow-Up _____
_____

© Teacher's Friend

A NOTE HOME TO PARENTS

Student _____

Date _____

Dear Parents

_____

_____

_____

_____

_____

_____

_____

_____

Teacher's Signature _____

Parents' Reply

☐ Please comment, and have your child return this lower section to the teacher.

☐ No need to respond.

☐ Reply received _____ (date)

☐ No reply received

☐ _____

☐ Second note sent home.

☐ Telephone call made _____ (date)

☐ Home visit _____ (date)

Teacher's Comment _____

Teacher's Follow-Up _____

A NOTE HOME TO
PARENTS

Student _____

Date _____

Dear Parents:

_____

Teacher's Signature

- -

Parent's Reply

☐ Please comment, and have your child return this lower section to the teacher.

☐ No need to respond.

_____

_____

_____

_____

_____

Parent's Signature

Date

A NOTE HOME TO PARENTS

Student _____ Date _____

Dear Parents:

_____

Teacher's Signature _____

Parent's Reply

☐ Please comment and have your child return this lower section to the teacher.

☐ No need to respond.

_____

Parent's Signature _____ Date _____

A NOTE HOME TO PARENTS

Student _____   Date _____

Dear Parents: _____

_____

_____

_____

_____

_____

_____

_____

_____

_____   **Teacher's Signature**

- -

Parent's Reply

☐ Please comment, and have your child return this lower section to the teacher.

☐ No need to respond.

_____

☐ Reply received _____ (date)   ☐ Second note sent home.

☐ No reply received.   ☐ Telephone call made _____ (date)

☐ _____   ☐ Home visit _____ (date)

Teacher's Comment _____

_____

Teacher's Follow-Up _____

_____

A NOTE HOME TO PARENTS

Student _____ Date _____

Dear Parents:

_____

_____

_____

_____

_____

_____

_____

Teacher's Signature _____

Parent's Reply

[ ] Please comment and have your child return this lower section to the teacher.

[ ] No need to respond.

[ ] Reply received _____ (date)

[ ] No reply received.

[ ] _____

[ ] Second note sent home.

[ ] Telephone call made.

[ ] Home visit. _____ (date)

Teacher's Comment _____

Teacher's Follow-Up _____

A NOTE HOME TO
PARENTS

Student _____ **Date** _____

Dear Parents:

_____ _____

Teacher's Signature

- -

Parent's Reply

☐ Please comment, and have your child return this lower section to the teacher.

☐ No need to respond.

_____

_____

_____

_____

_____

Parent's Signature _____ **Date** _____

A NOTE HOME TO PARENTS

Student _____ Date _____

Dear Parents:

_____ Teacher's Signature

Parent's Reply

☐ Please comment, and have your child return this lower section to the teacher.

☐ No need to respond.

Parent's Signature _____ Date _____

A NOTE HOME TO
PARENTS

Student _____ **Date** _____

Dear Parents: _____

_____

_____

_____

_____

_____

_____

_____

_____

_____

_____ **Teacher's Signature**

- -

Parent's Reply

☐ Please comment, and have your child return this lower section to the teacher.

☐ No need to respond.

☐ Reply received _____ (date)

☐ No reply received.

☐ _____

☐ Second note sent home.

☐ Telephone call made _____ (date)

☐ Home visit _____ (date)

Teacher's Comment _____

Teacher's Follow-Up _____

A NOTE HOME TO PARENTS

Student _____

Date _____

Dear Parents:

_____

_____

_____

_____

_____

_____

Teacher's Signature _____

Parent's Reply

☐ Please comment and have your child return this lower section to the teacher.

☐ No need to respond.

_____

_____

☐ Reply received _____ (date)

☐ No reply received

☐

Teacher's Comment _____

☐ Second note sent home _____ (date)

☐ Telephone call made _____ (date)

☐ Home visit _____ (date)

Teacher's Follow-Up _____

_____

A NOTE HOME TO
PARENTS

Student _____

Date _____

Dear Parents:

_____

Teacher's Signature

- -

Parent's Reply

☐ Please comment, and have your child return this lower section to the teacher.

☐ No need to respond.

_____

_____

_____

_____

_____

Parent's Signature _____

Date _____

A NOTE HOME TO PARENTS

Student _____   Date _____

Dear Parents:

_____

Teacher's Signature

☐ **Parent's Reply**   Please comment, and have your child return this lower portion to the teacher.

☐   No need to respond.

_____

_____

_____

_____

Parent's Signature _____   Date _____

A NOTE HOME TO
PARENTS

_____   _____
Student   **Date**

Dear Parents: _____

_____

_____

_____

_____

_____

_____

_____

_____

_____   _____

                                        Teacher's Signature

- -

Parent's Reply

☐ Please comment, and have your child return this lower section to the teacher.

☐ No need to respond.

_____

☐ Reply received _____ (date)   ☐ Second note sent home.

☐ No reply received.   ☐ Telephone call made _____ (date)

☐ _____   ☐ Home visit _____ (date)

Teacher's Comment _____

_____

Teacher's Follow-Up _____

_____

A NOTE HOME TO PARENTS

Student _____ Date _____

Dear Parents:

_____

_____

_____

_____

_____

_____

_____

_____

_____

Teacher's Signature _____

Parent's Reply

☐ Please comment, and have your child return this lower section to the teacher.

☐ No need to respond.

☐ Reply received _____ (date)

☐ No reply received.

☐ _____

☐ Second note sent home.

☐ Telephone call made. _____ (date)

☐ Home visit. _____ (date)

Teacher's Comment _____

Teacher's Follow-Up _____

_____

A NOTE HOME TO
PARENTS

_____   _____
Student   **Date**

Dear Parents:

_____   _____
                            Teacher's Signature

- -

Parent's Reply   ☐ Please comment, and have your child
                        return this lower section to the teacher.

                     ☐ No need to respond.

_____

_____

_____

_____

_____   _____
Parent's Signature   **Date**

© Teacher's Friend

A NOTE HOME TO PARENTS

Student _____

Date _____

Dear Parents:

_____

Teacher's Signature _____

Parent's Reply

☐ Please comment and have your child return this lower section to his teacher.

☐ No need to respond.

_____

Parent's Signature _____ Date _____

A NOTE HOME TO
PARENTS

Student _____   Date _____

Dear Parents: _____

_____

_____

_____

_____

_____

_____

_____

_____

_____

_____
Teacher's Signature

Parent's Reply

☐ Please comment, and have your child return this lower section to the teacher.

☐ No need to respond.

_____

☐ Reply received _____ (date)
☐ No reply received.
☐ _____

☐ Second note sent home.
☐ Telephone call made _____ (date)
☐ Home visit _____ (date)

Teacher's Comment _____

_____

Teacher's Follow-Up _____

_____

A NOTE HOME TO PARENTS

Student _____ Date _____

Dear Parents:

_____

_____

_____

_____

_____

_____

Teacher's Signature _____

Parent's Reply

☐ Please comment, and have your child return this lower section to the teacher.

☐ No need to respond.

☐ Reply received _____ (date)
☐ No reply received
☐ _____

☐ Second note sent home _____
☐ Telephone call made _____ (date)
☐ Home visit _____ (date)

Teacher's Comment _____

_____

Teacher's Follow-Up _____

_____

A NOTE HOME TO
PARENTS

Student _____   **Date** _____

Dear Parents:

_____

Teacher's Signature

- -

Parent's Reply

☐ Please comment, and have your child return this lower section to the teacher.

☐ No need to respond.

_____

_____

_____

_____

_____

Parent's Signature _____   **Date** _____

A NOTE HOME TO PARENTS

Student _____ Date _____

Dear Parents,

Teacher's Signature

Parent's Reply

☐ Please comment, and have your child return this lower section to the teacher.

☐ No need to respond.

A NOTE HOME TO

Parent's Signature _____ Date _____

A NOTE HOME TO
PARENTS

Student _____ **Date** _____

Dear Parents: _____

_____

_____

_____

_____

_____

_____

_____

_____

_____ **Teacher's Signature**

Parent's Reply

☐ Please comment, and have your child return this lower section to the teacher.

☐ No need to respond.

☐ Reply received _____ (date)

☐ No reply received.

☐ _____

☐ Second note sent home.

☐ Telephone call made _____ (date)

☐ Home visit _____ (date)

Teacher's Comment _____

_____

Teacher's Follow-Up _____

_____

© Teacher's Friend

A NOTE HOME TO PARENTS

Student _____   Date _____

Dear Parents:

_____

_____

_____

_____

_____

_____

_____

_____

_____
Teacher's Signature

Parent's Reply

☐ Please comment and have your child return this lower section to the teacher.

☐ No need to respond.

☐ Reply received _____ (date)

☐ No reply received

☐ _____

☐ Second note sent home.

☐ Telephone call made _____ (date)

☐ Home visit _____ (date)

Teacher's Comment _____

Teacher's Follow-Up _____

_____

A NOTE HOME TO PARENTS

Student _____ **Date** _____

Dear Parents:

_____ **Teacher's Signature**

Parent's Reply

☐ Please comment, and have your child return this lower section to the teacher.

☐ No need to respond.

_____

_____

_____

_____

Parent's Signature _____ **Date** _____

A NOTE HOME TO PARENTS

Student _____   Date

Dear Parents: _____

_____

_____

_____

_____

_____

_____

_____

_____

_____   **Teacher's Signature**

- -

Parent's Reply

☐ Please comment, and have your child return this lower section to the teacher.

☐ No need to respond.

_____

☐ Reply received _____ (date)   ☐ Second note sent home.
☐ No reply received.   ☐ Telephone call made _____ (date)
☐ _____   ☐ Home visit _____ (date)

Teacher's Comment _____

_____

Teacher's Follow-Up _____

_____

A NOTE HOME TO PARENTS

Student _____

Date _____

Dear Parents:

_____
_____
_____
_____
_____
_____
_____

Teacher's Signature _____

Parent's Reply

☐ Please comment, and have your child
    return this lower portion to the teacher.
☐ No need to respond.

☐ Reply received _____ (date)
☐ No reply received
☐

Teacher's Comment _____

☐ Second note sent home
☐ Telephone call made _____ (date)
☐ Home visit _____ (date)

Teacher's Follow-Up _____
_____

© Teacher's Friend

A NOTE HOME TO
PARENTS

_____   _____
Student   **Date**

Dear Parents:

_____
Teacher's Signature

- -

Parent's Reply

☐ Please comment, and have your child return this lower section to the teacher.

☐ No need to respond.

_____

_____

_____

_____

_____

_____   _____
Parent's Signature   **Date**

A NOTE HOME TO PARENTS

Student _____ Date _____

Dear Parents:

_____ Teacher's Signature

Parent's Reply

☐ Please comment and have your child return this lower section to me.

☐ No need to respond.

_____ Parent's Signature _____ Date

A NOTE HOME TO PARENTS

Student _____ **Date** _____

Dear Parents: _____

_____

_____

_____

_____

_____

_____

_____

_____

_____

Teacher's Signature

Parent's Reply

☐ Please comment, and have your child return this lower section to the teacher.

☐ No need to respond.

☐ Reply received _____ (date)

☐ No reply received.

☐ _____

☐ Second note sent home.

☐ Telephone call made _____ (date)

☐ Home visit _____ (date)

Teacher's Comment _____

_____

Teacher's Follow-Up _____

_____

A NOTE HOME TO PARENTS

Student _____ Date _____

Dear Parents:

_____

_____

_____

_____

_____

_____

_____

_____

_____

_____

Teacher's Signature _____

Parent's Reply

☐ Please comment and have your child
   return this lower section to the teacher.

☐ No need to respond.

☐ Reply received _____ (date)

☐ No reply received

☐ _____

☐ Second note sent home.

☐ Telephone call made _____ (date)

☐ Home visit _____ (date)

Teacher's Comment _____

Teacher's Follow-Up _____

A NOTE HOME TO PARENTS

_____   _____
Student   **Date**

Dear Parents:

_____   _____
                               Teacher's Signature

- -

Parent's Reply

☐ Please comment, and have your child return this lower section to the teacher.

☐ No need to respond.

_____

_____

_____

_____

_____

_____   _____
Parent's Signature   **Date**

© Teacher's Friend

A NOTE HOME TO PARENTS

Student _____ Date _____

Dear Parents:

_____

Teacher's Signature _____

Parent's Reply

☐ Please comment, and have your child return this lower section to the teacher.

☐ No need to respond.

_____

Parent's Signature _____ Date _____

A NOTE HOME TO
PARENTS

Student _____ **Date** _____

Dear Parents: _____

_____

_____

_____

_____

_____

_____

_____

_____

_____   _____
                          Teacher's Signature

Parent's Reply

☐ Please comment, and have your child return this lower section to the teacher.

☐ No need to respond.

_____

☐ Reply received _____ (date)

☐ No reply received.

☐ _____

☐ Second note sent home.

☐ Telephone call made _____ (date)

☐ Home visit _____ (date)

Teacher's Comment _____

_____

Teacher's Follow-Up _____

_____

A NOTE HOME TO PARENTS

Student _____

Date _____

Dear Parents: _____

_____

_____

_____

_____

_____

_____

_____

_____

Teacher's Signature _____

Parent's Reply

☐ Please comment, and have your child return this lower section to the teacher

☐ No need to respond.

_____

_____

☐ Reply received _____ (date)

☐ No reply received

☐ _____

☐ Second note sent home _____

☐ Telephone call made _____ (date)

☐ Home visit _____ (date)

Teacher's Comment _____

_____

Teacher's Follow-Up _____

_____

© Teacher's Name

A NOTE HOME TO
PARENTS

Student _____ Date _____

Dear Parents:

_____ Teacher's Signature

- -

Parent's Reply

☐ Please comment, and have your child return this lower section to the teacher.

☐ No need to respond.

_____

_____

_____

_____

_____

Parent's Signature _____ Date _____

A NOTE HOME TO PARENTS

Student _____ Date _____

Dear Parents:

Teacher's Signature _____

Parent's Reply

☐ Please comment, and have your child return this lower section to the teacher.

☐ No need to respond

Parent's Signature _____ Date _____

A NOTE HOME TO PARENTS

Student _____   **Date** _____

Dear Parents: _____

_____

_____

_____

_____

_____

_____

_____

_____

_____

Teacher's Signature

Parent's Reply

☐ Please comment, and have your child return this lower section to the teacher.

☐ No need to respond.

_____

☐ Reply received _____ (date)

☐ No reply received.

☐ _____

☐ Second note sent home.

☐ Telephone call made _____ (date)

☐ Home visit _____ (date)

Teacher's Comment _____

_____

Teacher's Follow-Up _____

_____

A NOTE HOME TO PARENTS

Student _____ Date _____

Dear Parents:

_____

_____

_____

_____

_____

_____

_____

_____

Teacher's Signature _____

Parent's Reply

☐ Please comment, and have your child
   return this lower section to the teacher.

☐ No need to respond.

☐ Reply received _____ ☐ Second note sent home _____
   (date)   ☐ Telephone call made _____
☐ No reply received   (date)
☐ _____ ☐ Home visit _____

Teacher's Comment _____

_____

Teacher's Follow-Up _____

_____

© Teacher's Friend

A NOTE HOME TO
PARENTS

Student _____   **Date** _____

Dear Parents:

_____   _____

Teacher's Signature

- -

Parent's Reply   ☐ Please comment, and have your child return this lower section to the teacher.

☐ No need to respond.

_____

_____

_____

_____

_____

_____   _____

Parent's Signature   **Date**

A NOTE HOME TO PARENTS

Student _____ Date _____

Dear Parents,

Teacher's Signature _____

Parent's Reply

☐ Please comment and have your child return this lower section to the teacher.

☐ No need to respond

Parent's Signature _____ Date _____

A NOTE HOME TO
PARENTS

Student _____ **Date** _____

Dear Parents: _____

_____

_____

_____

_____

_____

_____

_____

_____

_____

_____   **Teacher's Signature** _____

Parent's Reply

☐ Please comment, and have your child return this lower section to the teacher.

☐ No need to respond.

☐ Reply received _____ (date)

☐ No reply received.

☐ _____

☐ Second note sent home.

☐ Telephone call made _____ (date)

☐ Home visit _____ (date)

Teacher's Comment _____

_____

Teacher's Follow-Up _____

_____

A NOTE HOME TO PARENTS

Student _____ Date _____

Dear Parents:

_____

_____

_____

_____

_____

_____

_____

_____

_____

Teacher's Signature _____

Parent's Reply

☐ Please comment, and have your child return this lower section to the teacher.

☐ No need to respond.

☐ Reply received _____ (date)
☐ No reply received •
☐ _____

☐ Second note sent home. _____
☐ Telephone call made. _____ (date)
☐ Home visit. _____ (date)

Teacher's Comment _____

Teacher's Follow-Up _____

A NOTE HOME TO
PARENTS

Student _____

Date _____

Dear Parents:

_____

Teacher's Signature

- -

Parent's Reply

☐ Please comment, and have your child return this lower section to the teacher.

☐ No need to respond.

_____

Parent's Signature _____ **Date** _____

© Teacher's Friend

A NOTE HOME TO
PARENTS

Student _____ Date _____

Dear Parents,

Teacher's Signature _____

Parent's Reply

☐ Please comment, and have your child
   return this lower section to the teacher.

☐ No need to respond.

A NOTE HOME TO PARENTS

Parent's Signature _____ Date _____

A NOTE HOME TO
PARENTS

Student _____ **Date** _____

Dear Parents: _____

_____

_____

_____

_____

_____

_____

_____

_____

_____

_____ **Teacher's Signature**

Parent's Reply

☐ Please comment, and have your child return this lower section to the teacher.

☐ No need to respond.

☐ Reply received _____ (date)
☐ No reply received.
☐ _____

☐ Second note sent home.
☐ Telephone call made _____ (date)
☐ Home visit _____ (date)

Teacher's Comment _____

_____

Teacher's Follow-Up _____

_____

A NOTE HOME TO PARENTS

Student _____ Date _____

Dear Parents:

_____

_____

_____

_____

_____

_____

_____

_____

Teacher's Signature _____

Parent's Reply

☐ Please comment, and have your child return this lower section to the teacher.

☐ No need to respond.

☐ Reply received. _____ (date)

☐ No reply received.

☐ _____

Teacher's Comment _____

_____

☐ Second note sent home. _____ (date)

☐ Telephone call made. _____ (date)

☐ Home visit. _____ (date)

Teacher's Follow-Up _____

_____

A NOTE HOME TO PARENTS

Student _____

Date _____

Dear Parents:

_____

Teacher's Signature

- -

Parent's Reply

☐ Please comment, and have your child return this lower section to the teacher.

☐ No need to respond.

_____

_____

_____

_____

_____

Parent's Signature

Date _____

A NOTE HOME TO PARENTS

Student _____   Date _____

Dear Parents:

Teacher's Signature _____

Parent's Reply

☐ Please comment and have you... return this lower section to the teacher.

☐ No need to respond.

Parent's Signature _____   Date _____

A NOTE HOME TO
PARENTS

Student _____ Date _____

Dear Parents: _____

_____

_____

_____

_____

_____

_____

_____

_____

_____

_____
Teacher's Signature

- -

Parent's Reply

☐ Please comment, and have your child return this lower section to the teacher.

☐ No need to respond.

☐ Reply received _____ (date)

☐ No reply received.

☐ _____

☐ Second note sent home.

☐ Telephone call made _____ (date)

☐ Home visit _____ (date)

Teacher's Comment _____

_____

Teacher's Follow-Up _____

_____

A NOTE HOME TO PARENTS

Student _____ Date _____

Dear Parents:

_____

_____

_____

_____

_____

_____

_____

Teacher's Signature _____

Parent's Reply

☐ Please comment, and have your child
   return this lower section to the teacher

☐ No need to respond

☐ Reply received _____ (date)
☐ No reply received
☐ _____

☐ Second note sent home
☐ Telephone call made _____ (date)
☐ Home visit _____ (date)

Teacher's Comment _____

Teacher's Follow-Up _____

A NOTE HOME TO
PARENTS

Student _____   Date _____

Dear Parents:

_____

Teacher's Signature

Teacher's Signature

Parent's
Reply

☐ Please comment, and have your child return this lower section to the teacher.

☐ No need to respond.

Parent's Signature _____   Date _____

© Teacher's Friend

A NOTE HOME TO PARENTS

Student: _____ Date _____

Dear Parents:

_____

_____

Teacher's Signature

Parents
Reply

☐ Please comment, and have your child return this lower section to the teacher.

☐ No need to respond.

_____

_____

_____

_____

Parent's Signature _____ Date _____

A NOTE HOME TO
PARENTS

Student _____   **Date** _____

Dear Parents: _____

_____

_____

_____

_____

_____

_____

_____

_____

_____

Teacher's Signature

Parent's Reply

☐ Please comment, and have your child return this lower section to the teacher.

☐ No need to respond.

☐ Reply received _____ (date)

☐ No reply received.

☐ _____

☐ Second note sent home.

☐ Telephone call made _____ (date)

☐ Home visit _____ (date)

Teacher's Comment _____

_____

Teacher's Follow-Up _____

_____

A NOTE HOME TO PARENTS

Student: _____ Date _____

Dear Parents:

_____

_____

_____

_____

_____

_____

_____

_____

_____

Teacher's Signature

Parent's Reply

☐ Please comment and have your child return this lower section to the teacher

☐ No need to respond

☐ Reply received _____ (date)

☐ No reply received

☐ Second note sent home

☐ Telephone call made _____ (date)

☐ Home visit _____ (date)

Teacher's Comment

Teacher's Follow Up

A NOTE HOME TO
PARENTS

Student _____ **Date** _____

Dear Parents:

_____

Teacher's Signature

Parent's Reply

☐ Please comment, and have your child return this lower section to the teacher.

☐ No need to respond.

_____

_____

_____

_____

_____

Parent's Signature _____ **Date** _____

A NOTE HOME TO PARENTS

Student _____ Date _____

Dear Parents:

_____

Teacher's Signature

Parent's Reply

☐ Please comment, and have your child return this lower section to his teacher.

☐ No need to respond.

Parent's Signature _____ Date _____

A NOTE HOME TO
PARENTS

Student _____ **Date** _____

Dear Parents: _____

_____

_____

_____

_____

_____

_____

_____

_____

_____   **Teacher's Signature**

- -

Parent's Reply

☐ Please comment, and have your child return this lower section to the teacher.

☐ No need to respond.

☐ Reply received _____ (date)
☐ No reply received.
☐ _____

☐ Second note sent home.
☐ Telephone call made _____ (date)
☐ Home visit _____ (date)

Teacher's Comment _____

Teacher's Follow-Up _____

_____

A NOTE HOME TO PARENTS

Student _____

Date _____

Dear Parents:

_____

_____

_____

_____

_____

_____

_____

Teacher's Signature _____

Parent's Reply

☐ Please comment, and have your child return this lower section to the teacher.

☐ No need to respond.

Student _____

☐ Reply received _____ (date)

☐ No reply received

☐

☐ Second note sent home

☐ Telephone call made _____ (date)

☐ Home visit _____ (date)

Teacher's Comment _____

Teacher's Follow-Up _____

A NOTE HOME TO
PARENTS

_____   _____
Student   Date

Dear Parents:

_____
                                    Teacher's Signature

- -

Parent's Reply   ☐ Please comment, and have your child
                         return this lower section to the teacher.

                      ☐ No need to respond.

_____

_____

_____

_____

_____

_____

Parent's Signature   **Date**

A NOTE HOME TO PARENTS

Student _____

Date _____

Dear Parents:

_____

Teacher's Signature

Parent's Reply

☐ Please comment, and have your child return this lower section to the teacher

☐ No need to respond

_____

Parent's Signature _____ Date _____

A NOTE HOME TO
PARENTS

Student _____ Date _____

Dear Parents: _____

_____

_____

_____

_____

_____

_____

_____

_____

_____

_____ **Teacher's Signature**

- -

Parent's Reply

☐ Please comment, and have your child return this lower section to the teacher.

☐ No need to respond.

_____

☐ Reply received _____ (date)
☐ No reply received.
☐ _____

☐ Second note sent home.
☐ Telephone call made _____ (date)
☐ Home visit _____ (date)

Teacher's Comment _____

_____

Teacher's Follow-Up _____

_____

© Teacher's Friend

A NOTE HOME TO PARENTS

Student _____ Date _____

Dear Parents:

_____

_____

_____

_____

_____

_____

_____

_____

Teacher's Signature _____

Parent's Reply

☐ Please comment, and have your child return this lower section to the teacher

☐ No need to respond

☐ Reply received _____ (date)

☐ No reply received

☐ _____

☐ Second note sent home

☐ Telephone call made _____ (date)

☐ Home visit _____ (date)

Teacher's Comment _____

Teacher's Follow-Up _____

© Teacher's Friend

A NOTE HOME TO
PARENTS

Student _____

Date _____

Dear Parents:

_____

Teacher's Signature

- -

Parent's Reply

☐ Please comment, and have your child return this lower section to the teacher.

☐ No need to respond.

_____

_____

_____

_____

_____

Parent's Signature _____

Date _____

A NOTE HOME TO
PARENTS

Student _____ Date _____

Dear Parents:

Teacher's Signature _____

Parent's
Reply

☐ Please comment and have your child
   return this lower section to the teacher.

☐ No need to respond.

Parent's Signature _____ Date _____

A NOTE HOME TO
PARENTS

Student _____ Date _____

Dear Parents: _____

_____

_____

_____

_____

_____

_____

_____

_____ Teacher's Signature

- -

Parent's Reply

☐ Please comment, and have your child return this lower section to the teacher.

☐ No need to respond.

☐ Reply received _____ (date)
☐ No reply received.
☐ _____

☐ Second note sent home.
☐ Telephone call made _____ (date)
☐ Home visit _____ (date)

Teacher's Comment _____

_____

Teacher's Follow-Up _____

_____

A NOTE HOME TO PARENTS

Student _____

Date _____

Dear Parents:

_____

_____

_____

_____

_____

_____

_____

Teacher's Signature _____

Parent's Reply

☐ Please comment. And have your child return this lower section to the teacher.

☐ No need to respond.

_____

☐ Reply received. _____ (date)

☐ No reply received.

☐ Second note sent home.

☐ Telephone call made. _____ (date)

☐ Home visit. _____ (date)

Teacher's Comment _____

Teacher's Follow-Up _____

A NOTE HOME TO
PARENTS

Student _____ **Date** _____

Dear Parents:

_____ **Teacher's Signature**

- -

Parent's Reply

☐ Please comment, and have your child return this lower section to the teacher.

☐ No need to respond.

_____

_____

_____

_____

_____

_____

Parent's Signature _____ **Date** _____

A NOTE HOME TO PARENTS

Student _____ Date _____

Dear Parents:

_____

Teacher's Signature _____

Parent's Reply

☐ Please comment, and have your child
   return the lower section to the teacher.

☐ No need to respond.

_____

Parent's Signature _____ Date _____

A NOTE HOME TO
PARENTS

Student _____ **Date** _____

Dear Parents: _____

_____

_____

_____

_____

_____

_____

_____

_____

_____

_____   **Teacher's Signature**

Parent's Reply

☐ Please comment, and have your child return this lower section to the teacher.

☐ No need to respond.

_____

☐ Reply received _____ (date)   ☐ Second note sent home.

☐ No reply received.   ☐ Telephone call made _____ (date)

☐ _____   ☐ Home visit _____ (date)

Teacher's Comment _____

_____

Teacher's Follow-Up _____

_____

A NOTE HOME TO PARENTS

Student: _____ Date _____

Dear Parents:

_____

_____

_____

_____

_____

_____

_____

_____

_____
Teacher's Signature

Parent's Reply

☐ Please comment, and have your child
return this lower section to the teacher.

☐ No need to respond.

☐ Reply received _____ (date)   ☐ Second note sent home
☐ No reply received   ☐ Telephone call made _____ (date)
☐ _____   ☐ Home visit _____ (date)

Teacher's Comment _____

_____

Teacher's Follow-Up _____

_____

A NOTE HOME TO
PARENTS

Student _____   **Date** _____

Dear Parents:

_____

Teacher's Signature

Parent's Reply   ☐ Please comment, and have your child return this lower section to the teacher.

☐ No need to respond.

_____

_____

_____

_____

_____

Parent's Signature   **Date** _____

A NOTE HOME TO PARENTS

Student _____ Date _____

Dear Parents,

Teacher's Signature _____

Parent's Reply

☐ Please comment, and have your child return this lower section to the teacher.

☐ No need to respond.

Parent's Signature _____ Date _____

A NOTE HOME TO
PARENTS

Student _____ **Date** _____

Dear Parents: _____

_____

_____

_____

_____

_____

_____

_____

_____

_____

_____ **Teacher's Signature**

Parent's Reply

☐ Please comment, and have your child return this lower section to the teacher.

☐ No need to respond.

_____

☐ Reply received _____ (date)

☐ No reply received.

☐ _____

☐ Second note sent home.

☐ Telephone call made _____ (date)

☐ Home visit _____ (date)

Teacher's Comment _____

_____

Teacher's Follow-Up _____

_____

A NOTE HOME TO PARENTS

Student _____ Date _____

Dear Parents:

_____

_____

_____

_____

_____

_____

_____

_____

Teacher's Signature _____

Parent's Reply

☐ Please comment, and have your child return this lower section to the teacher.

☐ No need to respond.

☐ Reply received _____ (date)   ☐ Second note sent home.

☐ No reply received.   ☐ Telephone call made. _____ (a)

☐   ☐ Home visit _____ (h.v.)

Teacher's Comment _____

Teacher's Follow-Up _____

A NOTE HOME TO
PARENTS

Student _____ **Date** _____

Dear Parents:

_____   _____
Teacher's Signature

- -

Parent's Reply

☐ Please comment, and have your child return this lower section to the teacher.

☐ No need to respond.

_____

_____

_____

_____

_____

_____

Parent's Signature _____ **Date** _____

A NOTE HOME TO PARENTS

Student _____ Date _____

Dear Parents:

Teacher's Signature _____

Parent's Reply

- [ ] Please comment, and have your child return this lower section to the teacher.
- [ ] No need to respond.

Parent's Signature _____ Date _____

A NOTE HOME TO
PARENTS

Student _____ Date _____

Dear Parents: _____

_____

_____

_____

_____

_____

_____

_____

_____

_____

_____

Teacher's Signature

- -

Parent's Reply

☐ Please comment, and have your child return this lower section to the teacher.

☐ No need to respond.

_____

☐ Reply received _____ (date)
☐ No reply received.
☐ _____

☐ Second note sent home.
☐ Telephone call made _____ (date)
☐ Home visit _____ (date)

Teacher's Comment _____

_____

Teacher's Follow-Up _____

_____

A NOTE HOME TO PARENTS

Student _____ Date _____

Dear Parents:

_____

_____

_____

_____

_____

_____

_____

_____

Teacher's Signature _____

Parent's Reply

☐ Please comment, and have your child return this lower section to the teacher.

☐ No need to respond.

_____

_____

_____

Teacher's Comment _____

_____

Teacher's Follow-Up _____

_____

☐ Reply received _____ (date)   ☐ Second note sent home _____
☐ No reply received   ☐ Telephone call made _____ (date)
☐   ☐ Home visit _____ (date)

A NOTE HOME TO PARENTS

Student _____   **Date** _____

Dear Parents:

_____   _____

Teacher's Signature

- -

Parent's Reply

☐ Please comment, and have your child return this lower section to the teacher.

☐ No need to respond.

_____

_____

_____

_____

_____

Parent's Signature _____   **Date** _____

A NOTE HOME TO PARENTS

Student _____ Date _____

Dear Parents:

_____

Teacher's Signature _____

Parent's Reply

☐ Please comment, and have your child return this lower section to the teacher.

☐ No need to respond.

_____

Parent's Signature _____ Date _____

A NOTE HOME TO
PARENTS

Student _____ **Date** _____

Dear Parents: _____

_____

_____

_____

_____

_____

_____

_____

_____

_____

Teacher's Signature

Parent's Reply

☐ Please comment, and have your child return this lower section to the teacher.

☐ No need to respond.

_____

☐ Reply received _____ (date)

☐ No reply received.

☐ _____

☐ Second note sent home.

☐ Telephone call made _____ (date)

☐ Home visit _____ (date)

Teacher's Comment _____

_____

Teacher's Follow-Up _____

_____

A NOTE HOME TO PARENTS

Student _____ Date _____

Dear Parents:

_____

_____

_____

_____

_____

_____

_____
Teacher's Signature

Parent's Reply

☐ Please comment, and have your initial... return this lower section to the teacher.

☐ No need to respond.

☐ Reply received _____ (date)

☐ No reply received

☐

☐ Second note sent home.

☐ Telephone call made _____

☐ Home visit _____ (date)

Teacher's Comment _____

_____

Teacher's Follow-Up _____

_____

A NOTE HOME TO
PARENTS

Student _____   **Date** _____

Dear Parents:

_____

Teacher's Signature

 **Parent's Reply**

☐ Please comment, and have your child return this lower section to the teacher.

☐ No need to respond.

_____
_____
_____
_____
_____

Parent's Signature _____   **Date** _____

A NOTE HOME TO PARENTS

Student _____ Date _____

Dear Parents:

_____

Teacher's Signature

Parent's Reply

☐ Please comment and have your child return this lower section to the teacher.

☐ No need to respond.

_____

Parent's Signature _____ Date _____

A NOTE HOME TO
PARENTS

Student _____ Date _____

Dear Parents: _____

_____

_____

_____

_____

_____

_____

_____

_____

_____

_____ Teacher's Signature

Parent's Reply

☐ Please comment, and have your child return this lower section to the teacher.

☐ No need to respond.

_____

☐ Reply received _____ (date)

☐ No reply received.

☐ _____

☐ Second note sent home.

☐ Telephone call made _____ (date)

☐ Home visit _____ (date)

Teacher's Comment _____

Teacher's Follow-Up _____

_____